THE MAJESTY
OF THE MASS

Other works by Elizabeth Wang also published by Radiant Light:

Teachings-in-Prayer An Introduction.

Teachings-in-Prayer Volume One: Spiritual Training.

Teachings-in-Prayer Volume Two: Spiritual Nourishment.

Teachings-in-Prayer Volume Three: Spiritual Work.

Teachings-in-Prayer Volume Four: Spiritual Life.

Teachings-in-Prayer Volume Five: Spiritual Peace.

Living and Working for the King of Kings, Christ.

"My Priests are Sacred."

How to Pray (Part One: Foundations)

How to Pray Part Two: Liturgy and Morals.

Falling in Love: A Spiritual Autobiography.

Radiant Light: How the Work Began.

"Speak about Hope."

"Speak about Holiness."

An Invitation from Christ.

The Holy Sacrifice of the Mass: Mass Poster.

Radiant Light Conference Video 1999.

Radiant Light Conference Video 2000.

Radiant Light *books, paintings and posters are available to buy in person or by mail-order from:*

St Pauls (By Westminster Cathedral)
Morpeth Terrace, Victoria, London SW1P 1EP, UK.
Tel: 020-7828-5582; Fax: 020-7828-3329

Visit the Radiant Light web-site for an updated catalogue:
www.radiantlight.org.uk

THE MAJESTY OF THE MASS

WRITTEN AND ILLUSTRATED
BY ELIZABETH WANG

This book is published by ***Radiant Light***
25 Rothamsted Avenue
Harpenden, Herts., AL5 2DN, UK

First published January 2001

'C.C.C.' refers to the *'Catechism of the Catholic Church'*,
Geoffrey Chapman, London 1994, copyright © 1994
Geoffrey Chapman - Libreria Editrice Vaticana

Scripture quotations have been taken from the Jerusalem Bible
published and copyright 1966, 1967 and 1968
by Darton, Longman and Todd Ltd
and Doubleday & Co. Inc.

Text and illustrations by Elizabeth Wang

Text and illustrations copyright © Radiant Light 2001

Front cover design: detail from oil painting:
"The cup of My Blood"

ISBN 1-902960-31-9

"For this is what I received from the Lord, and in turn passed on to you: that on the same night that he was betrayed, the Lord Jesus took some bread, and thanked God for it and broke it, and he said, 'This is my body, which is for you; do this as a memorial of me.' In the same way he took the cup after supper, and said: 'This cup is the new covenant in my blood. Whenever you drink it, do this as a memorial of me.' Until the Lord comes, therefore, every time you eat this bread and drink this cup, you are proclaiming his death, and so anyone who eats the bread or drinks the cup of the Lord unworthily will be behaving unworthily towards the body and the blood of the Lord.

Everyone is to recollect himself before eating this bread and drinking this cup; because a person who eats and drinks without recognising the Body is eating and drinking his own condemnation." (1 Co 11:23-29)

CONTENTS

Section	Page
Introduction	i
Note	iii
The Mass from beginning to end: commentary with illustrations	1
1 INTROIT: Entry into the sanctuary	2
2 KYRIE: Lord, have mercy	4
3 GLORIA. Glory be to God	6
4 ALLELUIA: The Gospel	8
5 CREDO: The Creed	10
6 OFFERIMUS TIBI: The Offertory	12
7 SANCTUS: Holy, Holy, Holy Lord	14
8 EPICLESIS: Come, Holy Spirit	16
9 HOC EST: This is My Body	18
10 SANGUINIS MEI: The Cup of My Blood	20
11 MYSTERIUM FIDEI: The Acclamation	22
12 OMNES QUI: All our Departed	24
13 PER IPSUM: Through him, with him, in him	26
14 PATER NOSTER: Our Father	28
15 AGNUS DEI: Lamb of God	30
16 DOMINE: Lord, I am not worthy	32
17 COMMUNIO: Communion	34
18 LAUS ET JUBILATO: Praise and joy	36
19 ITE MISSA EST: Go, to love and serve	38
20 DEO GRATIAS: Thanks be to God	40
The Mass: Its six parts	43
The Mass: The saving Sacrifice	47
The Mass: Quotations from the Catechism	69
The Mass: Useful Scripture references	81

INTRODUCTION

In offering you a booklet of my 'Mass Paintings' I'd like to explain exactly what I was trying to capture when I painted each of the pictures which follow, and which can also be found on a Poster entitled: "The Holy Sacrifice of the Mass." So this is the story of their 'conception'.

About 1988, I was yearning more fiercely than ever to be able to share with other people my interest in the Mass, and in Our Lord, and in what He has done for us - and in what He still does today, sacramentally. Ever since I discovered the Catholic Church - and its principal act of worship - in the nineteen-sixties, I had been fascinated by Christ's Presence in the Blessed Sacrament.

I was only twenty-one and a half-hearted Christian when I discovered the truths at the heart of the Catholic Faith; and so I asked to be received into full communion. I had found, in finding the Catholic Church, the Divine institution which offers us all an authoritative and coherent body of teaching about God and mankind; and I had discovered that Jesus Christ our Lord is Really Present, in what is called sacramental form, in the tabernacle of every Catholic Church not only in this country but throughout the whole world.

I was so amazed, and thought it so marvellous, that I delved further into the Catholic Faith, throughout the years, always believing what the Church teaches, and trying to practise her teachings amidst the mixed joy and misery and muddle of everyday life 'in the world.' I learned through experience as well as through faith that the Church's teaching is indeed true. The Holy Eucharist is truly the source and summit of the Christian life (CCC:1323).

Throughout my adult life I continued to pray; and I also continued to paint: first, as an amateur and then as a professional artist who exhibited in London every summer. A great deal happened in the twenty-year gap between my reception into the Church and my attempts to paint the Mass; but my astonishment at Christ's Presence in the Holy Eucharist didn't lessen, nor did my gratitude lessen at being able to share, in the Church on Earth, in the eternal and glorious worship which is offered by all the Saints and Angels, through Christ, in Heaven: in union with the Holy souls as well: those of the Faithful Departed who are now passing through their purification.

So when I began the 'Mass Paintings' Series I tried to put down in paint what is really happening in our sanctuary during the Mass, with a glimpse of the majesty and Glory of the whole Church as it praises God with one voice. That's why a few of the paintings consist of a simple view of an ordinary part of the church or a procession, whilst others show what I know about the Consecration, for example, or Holy Communion or the Dismissal.

It was difficult to use oil paints again, when I'd spent years working in watercolour; also, the pictures were larger than my usual size; and so the work was done at home, in bits and pieces, fitted into my domestic routine. I used to sit in the kitchen, peeling potatoes, thinking about Christ in the Mass, and thinking about colour and tone; and then I'd pop into my studio for an hour or two to do a bit more painting, often working on five or six pictures at once.

The style was new to me; but it was a new venture and demanded a new style. I worked my way slowly forward for about two years and then decided to call a halt: I had so much other work to do.

The paintings have been exhibited in Westminster Cathedral, London, to encourage meditation, one Holy Week, and also in the Bar Convent Museum, York; and through these reproductions of my twenty oil paintings I continue to share what I know is a personal and of course limited view of the Mass; but I believe it's entirely orthodox. It is focused on Christ's Presence. I mean His presence amongst His People in the assembly, and also in His Minister: the priest, and in His Word in the Holy Gospel, and supremely, in an extraordinary manner, in the Holy Eucharist: which is the Blessed Sacrament: Christ's Sacred Body and Blood - and His soul and divinity; and so Christ is present 'whole and entire': our God, amongst us.

NOTE

The list of Scripture References, with the selection of quotations from the "Catechism of the Catholic Church," and the two-page list (on p. 43) of the six parts of the Mass, and the Section entitled "The Mass: the saving Sacrifice," are taken from "How to Pray Part Two," also written and illustrated by Elizabeth Wang, and published by Radiant Light in 1999.

THE MASS

FROM BEGINNING TO END

1. INTROIT: Entry into the sanctuary.

On every Sunday and holy day, or even daily, we gather before the sanctuary. Our church is a holy place, solemnly prepared for Catholic worship and sacrifice. That's why we face the holy altar, in which are enclosed, perhaps, the relics of some of the Saints who have lived and died for the Faith which we profess. Soon the priest will process to the altar and greet us warmly in the name of Christ our Lord.

Between the dark shadows in the painting a steady gleam indicates the presence of Christ in the tabernacle. He is truly God and truly man; and He is always Really Present here; and the best things we can do, as we approach Christ, are to make a reverent genuflection, and then to speak to Him from the heart, whether about special problems or special reasons for joy.

Christ is gladdened by our devotion. He loves to be with people who love Him, though He welcomes everyone who is here: whether they've arrived with love or curiosity, or anger or shame.

The nearby crucifix reminds us that our hope of real and everlasting joy comes through the Passion and Death of Christ. We are called to follow Christ in this life, on our journey towards Heaven - all the while loving God and our neighbour, and bravely shouldering our own crosses, and relying on Christ's help.

We can be sure of receiving help through our sincere participation in the Mass; and so we sacrifice a little of our time, first, to be united with Christ in the solemn offering which He makes to the Father, through the Church, from our altar, and then, if possible, to receive Christ in Holy Communion.

INTROIT: *Entry into the sanctuary.*

2. KYRIE: Lord, have mercy.

In the picture opposite, the light of God's Glory is shining out upon our hearts and lives, to enlighten and purify us and to free us from fear, when we're very aware of our weaknesses and failings. Sometimes our prayer-time is extremely painful, when we are penitent or ashamed. So here, at the beginning of the Mass, the worshippers seem to hesitate as God draws them to Himself. Many of us are aware of God's great holiness and our sinfulness. But we can remind ourselves that we are immensely precious to God.

If we've been aware of having committed serious sin, we've done well to combine humility with trust by confessing our sins to a priest in the Sacrament of Penance, or 'Confession': also called Reconciliation, in preparation for Mass and Holy Communion; yet everyone can show the same humility at the beginning of the Mass when we confess our little faults to God, confident that He forgives every weakness. Our faith is sure, because Christ speaks of mercy and forgiveness through His Church today, just as He spoke of them to His disciples.

By the Greek words which the Church has used for centuries - 'Kyrie eleison,' which means: 'Lord, have mercy' - we express our sorrow for our sins. We pause for a moment before we turn our attention away from ourselves, towards Christ our Saviour. This is the best way of preparing for the Sacred Mysteries in which we are about to take part. Despite our faults, as individuals, we are a Holy People who will offer the Holy Sacrifice of Christ from the altar.

We've gathered to celebrate Christ's Resurrection, and Ascension to Heaven, as well as His Passion and death; yet our joy is always mixed with reverence as we pray through, with and 'in' Christ to the Father, in the Spirit. We're not going to be just spectators but true children of God, lifting our hearts and minds to the Father in gratitude and simplicity, confident of receiving powerful gifts and graces.

KYRIE: *Lord, have mercy.*

3. GLORIA: Glory be to God.

Here, a small figure bows down in awe before the radiance and glory of God. Inwardly, we do the same as we prepare to recite the wonderful prayer of praise which begins: "Glory to God in the highest, and peace to his people on earth." This is where we leave behind our sorrow-for-sin and put aside thoughts about pain and failure. We are truly God's People. Each one of us is loved and cherished by Him more fondly and completely than we can imagine.

During the Sacred Liturgy - just as at home - we pray with our bodies as well as our hearts and voices; and whether we stand to pray, or kneel, or bow down before the Most Holy Trinity like the person in the picture, we're not grovelling, but adoring.

By Baptism, we have been made children of God; and if we love God, we're happy to worship Him. If we realise the truth about His Infinite majesty and goodness we love to genuflect, to bow, and to offer thanks and praise. Every good thing we possess is a free gift from God, and so it's only right to express our gratitude by reverent words and gestures.

By praying the Gloria we turn our hearts to the Father and to His Son: to the 'Holy One', Christ our Lord. We put our trust in Christ's merits, not our own. Through our union with Christ in Baptism and the other sacraments we hope to share in His holiness and to follow Him, our Way, to the Father.

GLORIA: *Glory be to God.*

4. ALLELUIA: The Gospel.

"Christ our Light": That's what we say at each Easter Vigil as we celebrate the Good News which the Church loves to share in every age. In dying for our sins, and then rising up from the grave, Christ has conquered sin and death; and we can share His life, if we belong to Him. We can be freed from fear and hopelessness by His Divine power.

The Light of the Gospel can be seen streaming out towards God's People, in the picture opposite, as the priest lifts up the book of the Gospels and invites everyone to venerate the Word of God. The figures on either side of the priest represent the holy Angels who throng the sanctuary; and the whole scene is bathed in light, since Christ the Word is present and alive at our celebration.

The Word of God is first honoured with prayers and incense. Then we prepare to hear this Word by making the Sign of the Cross on our foreheads, our lips, and our hearts. Silently, we ask the Holy Spirit to purify our thoughts, our words, and the desires of our hearts.

If we really love God, we want to be become holy temples for God, full of His truth, love and purity; and that's why we try to listen to God's Word with open, attentive hearts. That's how we can receive wisdom or warning, or joy and consolation. God will pour out His grace upon us during the readings from Holy Scripture, and will illuminate our hearts and minds with His wisdom and guidance.

God is at work during the whole of the Mass, whatever the weaknesses and limitations of the Clergy who offer the Holy Sacrifice - or of the laity who take part; and so we can be sure that in every reading from Holy Scripture, and in every homily, we can find a few words which are God's gift to us today: something especially suited to our present state and present needs.

ALLELUIA: *The Gospel.*

5. CREDO: The Creed.

Gathered together as one People before the sanctuary, we affirm our faith in the All-Holy God Who has revealed Himself through Christ by the Holy Spirit. The vivid streaks of colour opposite, in the sanctuary, are reminders of the power and majesty of our Creator. He is the God of Sinai - of Moses and Abraham - as well as the God of Bethlehem: Father of the infant Jesus.

Gathered together with our priest, we are glad to proclaim that we share one Faith: the Catholic Faith, handed down from the Apostles; and even if, as individuals, we feel that our faith is very weak, we believe that God can make us strong by the action of His grace in our hearts; and so we stand to celebrate the marvel of His love for us, reciting the Creed.

We list out loud the wonderful things that God the Father has done for us. He sent His Son to save us: Jesus Christ, Who was made flesh by the power of the Holy Spirit. It's as though we shout for joy together that we believe in the Most Holy Trinity, we believe in Christ our Incarnate God, born of the Blessed Virgin Mary, we believe in the Church and in God's mercy, and we believe in Heaven. And if we really believe these truths, we are longing to obey Christ and to keep His commandments, including His commandment to celebrate this Eucharist in His memory.

If we sincerely believe in Christ, we know that we can receive forgiveness and peace, through His saving work. It's through the sacraments that we receive the graces He won for us in His Passion. We have a sure hope of Heaven and salvation, if we remain true friends of Christ to the end of our lives; and meanwhile, if we have hopeful hearts and a true belief in God's love for each one of us we are able to see earthly situations and problems in their true perspective.

CREDO: *The Creed.*

6. OFFERIMUS TIBI: The Offertory.

After listening to the readings from Holy Scripture, we notice that representatives of the People of God bring gifts in procession. We know that everything we possess has come to us from the hand of God - food, drink, and our very lives; and so we approach the holy altar, in the presence of the Angels, to give everything back to God.

We offer not only bread and wine for the Holy Sacrifice, but our own selves as well: our joys, our works, our prayers, our sufferings, everything: as a sacrifice and an offering to God, so that His Will can be done in the world more and more, when we have been transformed and made holy, for His service and the service of our neighbour. We offer money too, sacrificing part of what we have earned or saved to support the Church, and to help the people she serves not only at home, but throughout the world.

Within a short time however, something really awesome is going to happen on the altar. The bread and wine which have been carried to the altar will soon be changed.

We are used to changes; after all, wheat and grapes have already become food and drink. But here, we look forward to something more extraordinary, when Christ will transform our gifts into His Holy Body and Precious Blood.

The priest washes his hands before us, symbolising his desire for purity; and we too - if we love God - increase our determination to lead good lives: to have pure hearts and intentions. If we allow ourselves to be transformed we will be divinised, that is, made God-centred and God-filled. We'll learn how to live for God's glory and not our own, wholeheartedly loving Him and our neighbour.

OFFERIMUS TIBI: *The Offertory.*

7. SANCTUS: Holy, Holy, Holy Lord.

In the picture opposite, it's as if God's holiness is like a pure furnace of love: Divine love, which overflows into open hearts.

We in the Church on Earth are very close to God at all times; but it's as though, during the Sacred Liturgy, we're on the 'brink' of Heaven's worship. The whole Church - of Earth, Heaven and Purgatory - is united with the holy Angels in praise of God the Holy Trinity.

Each generation of God's family has trembled with wonder before His Glory, praising His perfection in the prayer of the holy Angels, knowing - and perhaps fearfully aware - that nearness to God leaves no-one unchanged.

If we believe in God, we are awed by His holiness. We dare not, perhaps, think of the cost of serving Him; yet one of the great truths about God is that He never changes. He is love, as we read in Holy Scripture (1 Jn 4:8); and that Infinite love is always pouring out peace, mercy, forgiveness and many other gifts upon everyone who approaches in contrition and trust. God is so tender that He doesn't force us to serve Him; but He invites us to pray, and to grow in friendship with Him, and to prove our love by obedience and trust.

This is the moment in the Mass where we honour the mystery of the Most Holy Trinity, adding our voices to the praises of Heaven as we say: "Holy, Holy, Holy Lord, God of power and might. Heaven and Earth are full of your glory. Hosanna in the highest." (See Is 6:3)

SANCTUS: *Holy, Holy, Holy Lord.*

8. EPICLESIS: Come, Holy Spirit.

Now, the Liturgy of the Eucharist begins. All hesitation has gone. We belong here, true children of God, glad to be together before the altar; and as our priest calls out for the help of the Holy Spirit, we know that something of the Spirit's vision and aim and strength can be ours, provided that we trust in Him entirely.

God's Spirit has sometimes been seen as a dove. Here, the Holy Spirit is pictured not as the dove (Mt 3:16) which is mentioned in the Gospel story - when Jesus was baptised in the River Jordan - but as an eagle, to emphasise the Spirit's Almighty power. He is Almighty God: the Third Person of the Holy Trinity.

The Holy Spirit is already at work in our lives, prompting us to pray, opening our 'eyes' to truth, urging us to reach out to Christ's Church for sure teaching and for the grace which we can receive through the sacraments; and so we trust in the Holy Spirit's power, as we stand before the altar. We know that He will do, by His Divine power, what Christ, through His Church, asks Him to do.

After all our preparations, our priest now asks the Father (as in Eucharistic Prayer II): "Let your Spirit come upon these gifts to make them holy, so that they may become for us the Body and Blood of our Lord, Jesus Christ"; and so we ask the Holy Spirit to transform our gifts and ourselves as we prepare for the "Holy and perfect Sacrifice".

We can be sure that the holy Angels join our prayer, just as we joined theirs in the Sanctus; so it's worth making extra efforts to be attentive and prayerful, as we approach the most sacred part of the Mass.

EPICLESIS: *Come, Holy Spirit.*

9. HOC EST: This is My Body.

At last, the solemn prayer of consecration is recited devoutly by the priest. The sacred words of Christ are spoken, just as He spoke them at the Last Supper surrounded by His beloved Apostles. We hear our priest say: "This is My Body …" and then: "This is the cup of my Blood"; and we who believe in the constant teaching of Christ's Church know that Christ's Sacred body and Blood are Really Present on the altar, through the words and actions of our priest and the power of the Holy Spirit. Here, on the altar, is the Victim Who once died on Calvary: now here in sacramental form.

Christ is here: "wholly and entirely present" (CCC:1374): Body, Blood, soul and Divinity. He is gloriously alive now; and yet the picture opposite portrays Christ in His Passion, since He not only loved us and died for us on Calvary, but He also loves us and offers Himself for us now, in the Mass, as we take part in a living memorial of the Work of the Cross: of the saving Work of Christ.

He freely suffered the depths of pain and humiliation on the Cross, to save us from sin. This is the truth at the heart of our Faith: that Christ gave up His life for us, as His Mother stood close by, offering her only son; and God the Father has arranged, through His marvellous plan, that because we couldn't be there at Calvary, we can be here before the altar, participating in the Mass, as that very same sacrifice is offered today, at the hands of our priest.

All who welcome the truth - that Christ gave His life away as a ransom for us - welcome Christ's teachings and strive to follow His example. He is the Way to Heaven; and Heaven begins whenever we meet Him and do His Will - as did His holy Mother Mary. At every moment of her life she gladly consented to travel on her own Way of the Cross. She accepted the mystery of God's Will, just as we try to do. Even with all her holiness and special gifts she suffered in her efforts to remain faithful, and to persevere in hope and in love.

HOC EST: *This is My Body.*

10. SANGUINIS MEI: The Cup of My Blood.

In the image opposite, we can see the chalice which our priest holds up for everyone to see, after the consecration of the wine, which has now been changed into Christ's Precious Blood. What appears to be wine is now Christ's life-blood, which was once poured out on the Cross for the salvation of the world, for the sake of men, women and children of every century. Christ gave His very life-blood as reparation for our selfishness.

Christ died once on the Cross; yet because of what He has told us, we believe that here in the Mass, His one, Holy Sacrifice is solemnly re-presented: the sacrifice by which a New Covenant was made between God and mankind; and we fervently recall, in the Mass, not only Christ's sufferings, but also His glorious Resurrection and His Ascension into Heaven. Through Christ's work of Redemption we hope for salvation: for a real union with God - in this life by faith, and then face-to-face in the happiness of Heaven.

Outwardly, the Mass can look very simple; yet profoundly important things are happening. In this sacred memorial, the graces won for us by Christ on Calvary are applied - through our willing and sincere participation in the Mass - to us and to our lives: and also to the souls of the Faithful Departed. That's why we say that the Holy Sacrifice can be offered for 'the living and the dead'.

It's important for us to remember that after the consecration of the bread, which becomes the Sacred Body of Christ, and also after the consecration of the wine, which becomes the Precious Blood of Christ, Christ is present 'whole and entire' in each case. Although we cannot see Him, He is gloriously alive. He cannot be 'divided' into parts; and so we will receive Christ Himself - Body, blood, soul and divinity - later on, in Holy Communion, when we receive His Body (the Host) and when we receive His Precious Blood (from the chalice.)

SANGUINIS MEI: *The Cup of My Blood.*

11. MYSTERIUM FIDEI: The Acclamation.

It is by faith that we recognise Christ's silent and unseen Presence in the Blessed Sacrament. He is veiled from our sight; but what appears to be bread and wine is bread and wine no longer. Christ our Lord is here in Glory. His radiance fills the sanctuary. All the Holy Angels who share our worship can see this Glory, even though we are usually blind to it until we reach Heaven.

When we call out: "Christ has died, Christ is risen, Christ will come again" - or one of the other acclamations - we offer a great cry of gratitude. It's as though the whole Church is shouting out in joy and triumph because Christ has conquered sin and death, and has called us to live in unity as His Holy People. It's a real privilege to belong to Christ's Body on earth: to Christ's one, holy Church.

We have been reborn through Baptism, strengthened in Confirmation, forgiven - after our falls - in the Sacrament of Reconciliation, and made worthy to pray together for the Church and the world. Our High Priest is here, and we are His Priestly People. We can become 'one spirit' with Christ; and through the merits of His Holy Sacrifice we hope to share in His Resurrection and His Eternal Glory.

Before we reach Heaven, we really need the graces which we receive in our celebration of the Holy Eucharist. If we long to repay Christ's love for us with thanks and service we need His courage and wisdom and love; and if we are willing to share in His sufferings as we struggle to be faithful to Him during our life on earth we need His patience and compassion; and if we lean on Christ, rather than relying on our own strength, we can share in His mission too, despite our frailty. We can call others, by word or example, to "repent and turn to God" (Ac 3:19).

MYSTERIUM FIDEI: *The Acclamation.*

12.   OMNES QUI: All our departed.

In the painting, Christ reaches upwards to the Father, united in prayer with the Apostles, His friends. His Mother Mary and Saint John can be seen at one side; and it's as if we who take part in the Mass are about to come forward to join all these people who are looking up to Heaven.

We cannot reach the Father in prayer, by our own efforts; yet in the great prayer of the Church we join our little praises to Christ's perfect praise, to make one holy, perfect Offering, to the Glory of the Father, in thanksgiving for all gifts and graces, in reparation for sins, and in petition for help and salvation.

As we're gathered together, united in prayer, we ask that help be given not just to ourselves, but also to those in special need, and to the whole Church, including the Faithful Departed; indeed, our union with Christ joins us in a marvellous manner with everyone in the Church - including our brothers and sisters who have died but who have not yet been brought to the perfection of love. We offer Christ's sacrifice in reparation for their sins as well as our own.

Christ is quite rightly called the Way, since He alone links Heaven and earth; and when we walk in His way we reach out to everyone who lives in Him: people on earth and in Purgatory, and also the Saints in Heaven.

We venerate Christ's Holy Mother, who is with Christ in the glory of Heaven, by thanking God for her. We thank Him for all the tremendous Saints. We know that they all belong to us. They share in our joys, and they pray for us; and we honour them by our daily petitions and, supremely, by the great prayer of the Mass.

OMNES QUI: *All our departed.*

13. PER IPSUM: Through Him, with Him, in Him.

Next, our priest lifts up the chalice and paten, so offering Christ's Body and Blood, and saying: "Through him, with him, and in him, all glory and honour is yours, Almighty Father, for ever and ever." This is the summit of our celebration, as Christ draws us heavenward in His perfect prayer.

The Sacrifice now offered at the hands of our priest is a living memorial of Christ's Sacrifice of the Cross; yet as we remember His Death which He endured because of our sins we also celebrate His Resurrection and Ascension. It is the Risen Christ - the "living bread which has come down from Heaven" (Jn 6:51) - Who is amongst us, praying to the Father on our behalf, as the priest, like a visible Christ amongst us, reaches up to Heaven in prayer.

When we unite ourselves whole-heartedly to Christ's self-offering at Holy Mass we are like jewels on Christ's priestly robe. Christ transforms us by His grace. It's as though He makes us transparent so that His light can shine out in our lives. Each one of us belongs to Him, and each of us is really precious to Him, as He prays to the Father on our behalf: praying for our salvation - just as He prayed for us when He sacrificed Himself on Calvary.

Through Christ's perfect Sacrifice we offer worthy homage, thanksgiving and intercession to God our Father. With Christ our Lord we are united in one voice of praise of God's Glory. In Christ our Head we speak and act as One Body, praying in His love and power to the Father for everyone on earth, above all for the members of His Body: for His Holy Catholic Church. We all say "Amen": to signify that we too offer the Holy Sacrifice: united before the Father; and its important to remember that the whole Undivided Trinity - Three Divine Persons - is at work to help and save us through the power of the Mass, as the Father draws us all towards Himself, through Christ, by the Spirit.

PER IPSUM: *Through Him, with Him, in Him.*

14. PATER NOSTER: Our Father.

Christ is seen in the picture opposite as He stands in the midst of His brothers and sisters. But in the darkness of earthly life, they're all praying together. They're all aware, through faith, of the light and Glory of Heaven: just like us, when we stand together to pray the 'Our Father'.

At this point in Mass, it's almost time for us to make the sacrifice truly our own: by uniting ourselves with the Victim: with the living Christ, in Holy Communion. But we prepare for something as marvellous as that by acting like true children of God; and so we pray the 'Our Father': the prayer which Christ taught His first disciples (Mt 6:9-13). We're not ashamed to acknowledge our dependence on the God of love who made us and Who asks us to become as simple and as trusting as little children.

As we pray, we can remain aware that the Church teaches us that the Angels and Saints share our worship in a wonderful spiritual manner - even though we can't see them; and in their company we turn to our Father in Heaven to speak as children speak: to ask for help with open hearts. We make simple requests, trusting that God our Father will give us everything we really need.

Then we turn to one another, whether to strangers or family members, to offer a gesture of peace and a moment of true friendship. If we are closely united to other people, in a spiritual bond, by our faith in Christ, we have a special reason to love our neighbour with greater sincerity and gladness.

PATER NOSTER: *Our Father.*

15. AGNUS DEI: Lamb of God.

Christ wears a priest's garment, in the painting, since He is not only the "bread of life which has come down from Heaven"; and He is not simply our sacrificial 'lamb' and Victim. He is our High Priest, now alive and glorious; and so we pause before Him - the very Word made flesh - and say these ancient words in humility: "Lamb of God, have mercy on us … grant us peace."

As we speak, we see that the Bread of Life has been broken for our sake. We remember the terrible way in which Christ was stripped and sacrificed on the Cross: offered up like one of the lambs then being offered in the Temple sacrifices. Out of love for us, He has paid a terrible price for our salvation. By His blood, He has made a New Covenant between human beings and the Invisible God, the Almighty Father; and since it's a covenant sealed in the blood of the only Son of God, it is unbreakable.

As creatures who have been made by God it's as if, in one sense, we are 'dust' before Jesus, Who is true God and true man; but it's a cause for gratitude that He did not come to earth "to call the virtuous, but sinners" (Mt 9:13). We can be at peace in our frailty if we're determined to live as He wishes us to live, obedient to Him and to the Church which He founded and which He still guides today.

In His great love for us Christ rewards and comforts every contrite heart. Nothing can keep us from Him except sin, or fear, or stubbornness in disobedience and pride.

AGNUS DEI: *Lamb of God.*

16.   DOMINE: Lord, I am not worthy.

We cannot see Christ with our bodily eyes; but the painting reminds us that by our faith we can recognise Christ in the Blessed Sacrament in His majesty and power. The glory of Heaven streams from His holy face.

Christ is really present, Body, Blood, Soul and Divinity - a tremendous gift to us; but if we long to receive Him in Holy Communion, we pause before Him once again, admitting our unworthiness, and contemplating the wonder of what's about to happen. We can each have a personal, intimate meeting with Christ our God: our Creator, and Saviour, and friend.

Until now, we've been praying as one Body: God's People, gathered together to celebrate our 'Passover' from spiritual death to new life, and Christ's Passover from Earth to Heaven; yet in a private moment each of us can speak from the heart to the Saviour Who waits to greet us.

We're not worthy to receive Christ in Holy Communion; but He's thrilled to be amongst us, who love Him; and He loves to give joy: the sort of joy and peace that we can receive in no other way but through Him.

We can be sure that Christ gives a tender welcome to everyone who turns to Him. He is the "friend of ... sinners" (Mt 11:19); and that's why we trust Him as we try to grow closer to Him on our journey of faith. We can receive extraordinary hope through our encounter with the very One Who said: "To have seen Me is to have seen the Father" (Jn 14:9).

DOMINE: *Lord, I am not worthy.*

17. COMMUNIO: Communion.

There's a host of Saints and Angels close by us, in the church: rank upon rank of them, sharing our joy, as we make our way towards the sanctuary for Holy Communion. It's a bit like Galilee, when the crowds were struggling to be close to Jesus. But they could only touch Him, briefly. We can speak to Him and confide in Him, and enjoy His Presence.

It's as if Christ disguises Himself very humbly, so that we can go up to the sanctuary with hope in our hearts and not fear. He knows our struggles; and He wants us to welcome Him joyfully and with simple trust. We can take Him into our souls and lives; and in a mysterious way we feed on His Divine Life; and He draws us closer to His heart.

As we receive Him, there's a further reason for gratitude. Christ binds us closer to every member of His Church through our union with Him, our Head. Whatever the real or apparent differences between us, we all share, through Christ, a relationship which is closer than that which binds any earthly relations. We are really one body, members of Christ's One Body, on earth and in Heaven.

It sometimes happens that members of the Church - or other prayerful persons - cannot receive Holy Communion; but this should not lead to self-pity or anger; rather, whoever knows that he can't receive Communion can stay quietly praying where he is; and he can make a 'spiritual Communion' - by a brief expression of contrition, and of love for Christ, with a fervent request that Christ come to his heart with help and consolation.

Christ responds to such sincere prayers, because He is good; and so whoever prays in this way can make an act of faith in Christ's love for him, and also thank Christ and confide in Him, and so allow Christ to work real changes within his soul.

COMMUNIO: *Communion.*

18. LAUS ET JUBILATIO: Praise and Joy.

There's a moment after Holy Communion when each one of us can rest, alone with Jesus, in a peaceful prayer of thanksgiving. Here, a single worshipper kneels within the radiance of Three Persons in light. The truth of the Godhead is shown in symbols, to show that when Christ is Present in each soul in Communion He is not separated from the Father and the Holy Spirit. He is never separated from them.

The Three Divine Persons are One God, undivided; and we know that the Most Holy Trinity dwells within the soul of each baptised person who is in a state of grace; so when Christ comes to the soul in Holy Communion He draws the privileged communicant even more surely towards the heart of the Holy Trinity. This really happens, whether we seem to kneel in darkness, or whether we experience spiritual light and joy and consolation.

Christ is, all-at-once, our spiritual food, and our best and most loving friend. He longs to keep us close to Him and to give us His peace, immediately - and throughout our lives, and after our death as well.

In our Holy Communion we find a holy companionship which is offered to all who have been bound together in life and faith and worship within Christ's Holy Church. Here, we can glory in Christ's love and renew our faith in Him.

We can rest with Christ in silent companionship or speak from the heart about our hopes, our problems - our whole lives; or we can allow Him to lead us, should He choose to do so, into the 'heights' of prayerful union with Himself, whether to the sweet darkness of Unknowing or to the radiant light at the very 'edge' of Heaven.

LAUS ET JUBILATIO: *Praise and Joy.*

19. ITE, MISSA EST: Go to love and serve.

The fervour of Christ's People is expressed as candle-flame and fire, in the picture opposite. This is what the church is like, spiritually, when souls are ablaze with Divine Love: when each person is lit up with the Light of Christ.

The priest blesses everyone present, in the name of the Father and of the Son and of the Holy Spirit. He encourages us all to go out into the world, glowing with fervour and love, in imitation of Christ.

We mustn't depart only to busy ourselves with personal tasks and concerns. Christ wants us to love everyone for His sake, cheerfully: first family and friends; then neighbours, acquaintances and workmates - whether 'superiors' or 'juniors'. He asks us to love our enemies - all of them. He asks us to love the sick, the sad, the poor and the lonely, and to remember that we ourselves are frequently sick, sad, poor or lonely, before Christ, waiting for help.

In these Holy Mysteries we have proclaimed the Apostolic Faith. We now have the duty and privilege of preaching the Gospel by our words and example, bringing to other people the Good News about the forgiveness of sins and our hope of union with God. We must speak - even in weakness and suffering - about Christ and His sacraments, about prayer and trust, and about the joy and peace which He has freely given to us.

It should be our whole aim, after receiving Christ our God into our hearts, to tell other people about the hope, love and sense of purpose to be found through Christ and His Church. He wants us to go out not to pursue selfish ambitions, but to work, pray and celebrate in the various ways which will best fulfil His Will and will bring glory to the Father and help to other people.

ITE, MISSA EST: *Go to love and serve.*

20. DEO GRATIAS: Thanks be to God.

Peace reigns after Holy Communion. A worshipper kneels and bows low in gratitude and adoration. Here, the tall column of white Light represents this person's Guardian Angel: always nearby. A pure spirit has been given to each of us by God, to keep us from evil and to steer us towards Heaven.

The holy Angels share our daily lives as well as our worship. They guard and help us inside and outside our churches. Christ our Lord said that they worship God in heaven whilst they also guard His "little ones" on earth (Mt 18:10); and if we really believe that we are guarded by angels, fed by Christ, and wrapped in the prayers of His Holy Mother Mary and of all the other Saints, we'll never stop being grateful to God for our new life.

Nothing can defeat us if only we'll trust in Christ and not in ourselves. He never fails to answer our prayers - although He sometimes does so in unexpected ways; and so it's important that we ask Him, every day, for the grace to persevere in love, through the little problems or the horrible difficulties which we meet in our daily routine.

Perhaps we dash out straight after the final hymn, both to enjoy some of the good things available in our life 'in the world' and to share the Good News: that in our Communion with Christ and His Church we find new joy, hope, peace, and fulfilment. Or perhaps we remain in prayer for a few minutes longer, to offer another word of thanks to Christ - God within us. Those of us who believe in Him know that we've really heard "Good News" (Mk 16:15). Christ's Infinite loving-kindness has caused Him to come from Heaven to be amongst us: first, in His Incarnation just over two thousand years ago, and now daily - in sacramental form - every time He is made Present on our altar, in the Holy Sacrifice of the Mass.

DEO GRATIAS: *Thanks be to God.*

THE MASS

ITS SIX PARTS

THE HOLY SACRIFICE OF THE MASS: SIX PARTS.

1. THE INTRODUCTORY RITE.
(The whole Church of Earth, Purgatory and Heaven is involved in the Mass.)

    A WELCOME (by the priest)
    THE SIGN OF THE CROSS
    A SPRINKLING (with holy water)

2. THE PENITENTIAL RITE.
(We pause to repent of our sins.)

    THE "I CONFESS"
    THE KYRIE ("Lord, have mercy, Christ have mercy …")
    THE GLORIA ("Glory be to God on high …")

3. THE LITURGY OF THE WORD.
(Christ speaks to us by His living word.)

    THE READINGS, which are:
- 1st reading (Old Testament)
- Psalm
- 2nd reading (from the New Testament, but not from the Gospels)
- Holy Gospel (from one of the Four Gospels)

    THE HOMILY (Explanation of the Gospel message)
    AN ACT OF FAITH (The Creed)
    OUR INTERCESSIONS (Bidding prayers)

4. THE LITURGY OF THE EUCHARIST.

(Calvary's offering is re-presented. Christ is made present: "whole and entire.")

    THE PREPARATION OF THE ALTAR
    THE PROCESSION OF GIFTS
    THE EUCHARISTIC PRAYER, which includes:
- Thanksgiving (Preface)
- Sanctus ("Holy, Holy, Holy Lord …")
- Epiclesis (The Church asks the Father to send His Holy Spirit)
- Institution Narrative (Consecration of the bread and wine)
- Memorial Acclamation (A declaration of faith)
- Anamnesis (Christ's Passion is called to mind)
- Intercessions (for living and departed)
- Final Doxology (Through Christ we glorify the Father, in the Spirit)
- The great "Amen" (by which we unite ourselves to Christ's offering.)

5. THE RITE OF COMMUNION.

(Christ Himself is our spiritual Food)

    THE "OUR FATHER"
    THE PEACE OF THE LORD
    THE "LAMB OF GOD"
    THE FRACTION (Breaking of the Sacred Host)
    "THIS IS THE LAMB OF GOD"
    HOLY COMMUNION

6. THE CONCLUDING RITE.

(A preparation to carry the Gospel out to the world)

    ANNOUNCEMENTS
    THE BLESSING
    THE DISMISSAL

THE MASS

THE SAVING SACRIFICE

THE MASS

THE SAVING SACRIFICE

a) THE RECONCILIATION OF MANKIND WITH GOD.

A very costly sacrifice.

Have you noticed how some of the phrases we use most frequently seem to lose their power? It's very easy to chat about 'The Holy Sacrifice' or 'Calvary's Offering'; and yet our Redemption was effected through a very costly sacrifice. Only because of Christ's heroic and horrific death on the Cross, with His subsequent Resurrection and Ascension, have we been offered a way to Heaven; and that's why I want to describe the doctrine of our Redemption, a little at a time, in the briefest and easiest way, to clarify the subject …

We who belong to the Church and who believe in her teachings believe that Jesus Christ the Son of God died on the Cross to save us. We believe that He is our Redeemer, and that it's only because of what we call His redeeming work that the life of grace has been restored to us and our entry into Heaven made possible. But there are several theories about exactly how we were redeemed, or rather, about the exact meaning of the word 'Atonement'.

The Church requires us to believe in the fact of Mankind's reconciliation with God through Christ's death on the Cross, but we're not required to believe in St. Anselm's theory of Redemption, for example, rather than in someone else's. It's more important to know what Christ has done for us than how He did it: although every facet of the Redemption is fascinating, to those who long to know more about Christ. Yet the Church does not insist that we hold to one particular theory about exactly how Christ's saving work - His paschal work - proved effective. What I've written below, after thought, study and prayer, is what seems to me to be a reasonable explanation; and I hope that this all accords with the truths of Holy Scripture and of the Sacred Tradition ...

Anyone who wants to know the fuller meaning of rebellion against God, for example, or of Christ's Incarnation, has only to look at the relevant passage in the Catechism of the Catholic Church.

Disobedience.

If I must begin with the simplest-possible statement about our sinful human nature, and about what the Church calls *"the fall narrated in Genesis"* (CCC:388) I can say:

- Long ago, God gazed lovingly upon the world which He had created; but Mankind had rebelled; and every human being was estranged from God.

- Through His chosen people, and His prophets, God made preparations for the fulfilment of His marvellous plan to save us: but until that moment of fulfilment, Heaven was to remain 'shut'.

- By God's Will, an immaculate child was conceived in the womb of St. Anne: and that child was Mary: *"preserved immune from all stain of original sin"* (CCC:491).

- When grown into a woman, Mary remained pure in heart, and also remained the purest of all virgins. At her consent, God the Son took flesh from her, at His Incarnation, and so lay in her womb, until His birth, on Earth, as the sinless God-man who would save His People from their sins, that is, save those who would accept Him and would accept (as I will explain) what He would do for them.

- Jesus Christ the God-man came to Earth to sacrifice His life: to save sinners from the everlasting death and torment which are inevitable, if we remain eternally without God Who is the Source of Eternal joy.

- How did Christ sacrifice His life? First, by enduring, on Earth, all that a sinless person 'ought' not to have suffered: all the penalties, torments and repercussions of Mankind's original Fall, for example, the opposition and cruelty of sinful opponents, with the added difficulties of hunger and pain; and of course Christ was plagued by temptations; and he suffered heart-ache because of danger, fear, and disappointment or loss.

- Christ 'deserved' only to live in perpetual bliss; but He gladly endured all sorts of trials and torments as a sacrifice for our sake. He was living on Earth because He loves us; and He bore these things - though He hadn't sinned - because of His great love for us.

- But there was more.

Obedience: a virtue.

- The essence of Christ's sacrifice - all of His whole life's sacrifice - lay in the fact that He bore these things out of obedience to God the Father Who sent Him - His Son - to Earth.

- And what was mankind's sin? Disobedience. Christ the God-man, by His Infinitely-worthy sacrifice (of daily bearing unmerited sufferings) was 'cancelling out' - so to speak - the disobedience of His human brothers and sisters, as He lived amongst sinful people on Earth, praying for sinners, and doing the Father's Will in every detail.

- But there was more.

A perfect offering.

- God the Father foresaw that His Son, from love, would accept every and any suffering which He would encounter on Earth, and that He would encounter more suffering than most, since perfect Truth is viciously opposed by evil; and so the Father permitted, planned, foresaw, willed and accepted the pure sacrifice which His own Divine, spotless Son was to make of Himself from on Earth; and this sacrifice lay not only in the daily sufferings already mentioned, but in the Great Suffering, which was death itself. This was not 'due' to Christ, since He was sinless. It was 'undeserved' by any of His actions; yet it was accepted by Him, freely.

- Christ was willing to endure a difficult life and also a cruel death so that by His love and obedience 'during the enduring' on the Cross it was as though He was saying to the Father: "Accept this Act of obedience, this Holy Sacrifice, freely made by Me, Your Divine Son. Accept it as an offering made on behalf of my true brothers and sisters. Here I am amongst them: flesh and blood like them. Accept my love and obedience and forgive their lack of love and their lack of obedience. Accept the sufferings I endure now, especially death itself, which I do not 'deserve', as a Sacrifice - a penance - which I freely offer to You because of their sins. No sacrifice which they make alone can ever be penance enough to make up for their offences against your Divine Majesty".

- So: Christ's offering was accepted; and the unique sacrifice which He freely offered from the Cross infinitely surpassed in value the animal sacrifices which the Chosen People had traditionally offered through their priest in recognition of God's power and sovereignty and in reparation for their sins.

- Christ was the real, pure, spotless 'Lamb' of Sacrifice, Who offered Himself, from love, for the reasons given above. He really died on the Cross; yet because of Who He is He conquered sin and death. He rose from the grave; and when He had ascended to Heaven in glory, returning to the Father, it was as though He left 'open' the 'gate' of Heaven for all who would believe in Him, follow Him, remain faithful in His service, and so be made fit for Eternal Glory.

- It's important for us to know that Christ loves all Mankind. He died for all; yet His sacrifice can 'redeem' only those who are willing to accept Him and believe in Him, and who accept and are grateful for what He has done for them. It's because of God's immense respect for us that He doesn't force us to love and to respond to His love: indeed, a forced response can't properly be called love. That's why Christ, through His Church, invites us all to repent and to change. When we freely unite ourselves with Christ in the bond of love - usually through undergoing Baptism - we can therefore offer His Sacrifice for our own sins. We can claim His Sacrifice as our own.

- There seems to be a big problem, however. We know that very few people were beside Christ, as He died for sinners. How did it become possible for people like ourselves - and for people world-wide, and of many generations - to make Christ's Sacrifice our own? How is it possible for us all to plead beside Christ, before God the Father, and somehow to be associated with Christ's redeeming Act?

Calvary re-presented.

- We know from Sacred Scripture and from the Tradition that 'the just' who lived on Earth in the centuries before Christ's Incarnation were redeemed by Christ and made fit for Heaven; but they couldn't enter Heaven after their deaths until Christ, by His own death, had opened the Way back to the Father. This is why Christ 'descended to the dead' after His own death - as we profess in our Creed. He 'descended' in triumph: to share the Good News that the suffering and death which He had endured to redeem Mankind were now accomplished.

- Christ then rose from the dead, and in His glorified body appeared to many of His followers. He gave them further understanding and instruction, and then ascended into Heaven. Through His wisdom and love, He left behind an infant Church which was able to teach with His authority and to baptise all new believers. He sent His own Holy Spirit to His Church a few weeks after His Ascension, in order to guide and empower its members and to give special help to the Apostles and to their successors.

- Christ foresaw the needs of every generation which would be born on Earth between His own life-time and the end of time. In His wisdom and love, and even before His death on the Cross, Christ did what was necessary for men, women and children of future generations - and those of His own generation who remained on earth after His Ascension to Heaven - to be able to offer His Sacrifice for sins.

- **At the Last Supper, on the night before He died, Christ gave thanks for the bread and the wine before Him; and when He gave thanks for one and then for the other, He declared - of one, and then of the other - 'This is My Body' and later 'This is My Blood.' It was through this 'institution' of a living memorial of His saving work of the Cross that Christ bequeathed to His Church an astonishing gift. Through giving His Church the Holy Sacrifice of the Mass - the living memorial of His Passion - Christ made it possible for people of future generations to be present as He prays to the Father for their Salvation. When Christ instructed His Apostles, "DO THIS", as He consecrated the bread and wine and so changed bread and wine into His Body and Blood, He was giving to those men and to their successors, and to all His priests through many centuries, the power to effect that same change; and so we believe that at every Mass, in a sacramental way, Christ 'rejoins' us who are His present-**

day disciples; and He prays to the Father on our behalf. **Christ is Really Present amongst His disciples in every era of the Church; and so His offering of Calvary is re-presented before us, in our day. It is offered to the Father from our altar. Furthermore, this Eucharistic sacrifice culminates in a commemorative meal which we call "Holy Communion". We participants can receive the Body and Blood of Christ as our spiritual food; and in doing so we are intimately united with our Risen Saviour.**

The unique saving sacrifice, re-presented.

- Sad to say, it's so easy to take for granted the marvel which takes place daily in our churches. Every time the Holy Sacrifice of the Mass is offered by His Church, Christ makes His total self-offering to the Father. Christ is Really Present: Body, Blood, soul and Divinity, as we say: whole and entire.

- By the two-fold consecration of the bread and the wine, and the offering of Christ's Sacred Body and Precious Blood from the altar, His death is recalled and His once-for-all Holy Sacrifice is offered again, as an Offering of perfect homage to the Father, and as a sacrificial offering for the forgiveness of sins of the living and the departed.

- Christ is Really Present amongst His People in every generation. He is Present as our risen, triumphant Lord. He pleads on behalf of the living and the departed, as His Church offers her great prayer to the Father in Christ's Name.

- All that the Church prays for, in her liturgy, is requested by Christ of the Father, as the Spirit binds together in one prayer all who love Christ and who take part in the Mass.

- For a sincere participation by the laity in the Holy Sacrifice of the Mass, a sincere union-of-heart with Christ is even more important than a reverent recitation of the responses, although both are fitting, for the praise of God the Holy Trinity.

- **By joining in the offering of this One Holy, eternal Sacrifice of Christ, each repentant sinner present - or each person united to the Mass by desire, if kept away by duty, imprisonment or sickness - is as though saying to the Father: "I couldn't stand beside Christ on Calvary; yet I stand beside Him now, of my own free will, confessing my sins, believing in Him, and believing in the Sacrifice He once made on Calvary for my sake. With Christ, I offer that same Sacrifice to You now, Father, from this altar. Accept Christ's plea on my behalf. Save me from the consequences of my sin. Restore me to friendship with You. Bring me to Heaven, for the sake of Christ, to Whom I am united by baptism and by loyalty; and bring to Heaven, too, everyone present here and all of the people in my heart."**

- Thus, God the Father hears Christ's pleas on behalf of repentant sinners in this era. He looks joyfully upon all who cluster about Christ their Saviour, just as, nearly two thousand years ago, He gazed joyfully upon the sinful people who greeted Christ on Earth, believed in Him, turned away from sin, and followed in His footsteps.

---

b) CHRIST'S PRAYER FOR US.

A modern tragedy.

- How tragic it is that so few people today seem to hurry eagerly to the Holy Sacrifice of the Mass. So many people don't seem to know or care that something extraordinary takes place at every Celebration: and happens because of the sacrifice of Calvary, in which Christ was triumphant.

- Eager 'converts' have been awed and amazed to hear the 'Good News' that Calvary's sacrifice is re-presented at every Mass. Christ is pleading and praying for us all at every Mass: offering His one, perfect sacrifice in order to save us from estrangement from the Father Who is the Source of all true joy; and that's why obedient enquirers become incorporated into Christ's Body on Earth : the Church. That's why we try to make that sacrifice our own, weekly or even daily, through a union of heart, mind and will with Christ - and through receiving Him in Holy Communion.

Source of holiness and hope.

- For each repentant sinner Christ is not solely the Saviour Whose Resurrection and Ascension encourage us to hope for Heaven; nor is He merely a model for holy behaviour on Earth. He's also the Source of Divine life and grace through which we can hope to lead Divinely-holy, grace-filled and Christ-like lives. We realise that it's only by Christ's strength, not our own, that we can love and obey Him and His Church, as we try to do good and shun evil. Only because of the gifts we receive from Christ can we persevere on a narrow path, on a difficult yet holy pilgrimage, confident that He can lead us home to Heaven.

- How little is asked of us at each moment: only a little faith, a little sorrow-for-sin, a little determination to rely on Christ for the grace to change, and a little effort to stand before Him as His Holy Sacrifice is offered from our altar, at the hands of our priest.

- As God raised up and glorified the Divine, obedient Son, so He will raise up and glorify all who belong to Christ and who have remained faithful to the end.

- Other people have said: "Did Christ have to die? Couldn't He have saved us in some other way?" Yes, of course; He could have formed a different plan; but who would dare to say that His wise decision could have been improved upon?

- Isn't it extraordinary, that we're saved by One single extraordinary Act of love-even-to-death of the God-man, in a life which now is held us before us as an astonishing example? If we believe in a God Who loves sinful human beings so much that, for our sake, He endured undeserved suffering throughout His life on Earth, how can we fail to make efforts to bear our own sufferings in a way worthy of that Divine Saviour? How can we fail to be compassionate towards our suffering neighbour?

- Although as Christ's friends we will meet suffering and temptation, we can hope to avoid the worse sorts of sadness and spiritual danger which oppress all who don't know about Christ, or who don't know about His sacrifice for sin; and it's important that we make loving efforts to share our faith, and so bring hope to people who don't know that through the offering of the Holy Sacrifice of the Mass they make Christ's sacrifice effective for their own lives. It's very important to pray for people who don't care about Christ's sufferings, and to pray for all the discontented Catholics who begrudge an hour spent at Mass, in prayer, as Christ Himself, in the sanctuary, pleads for their salvation.

- What tremendous hope God has given to sinful people who believe in His love; and what astonishing gifts are offered by His Son, Our Saviour, at the Holy Sacrifice to which Christ calls us. Christ feeds us with His own Body and Blood. His entire, glorious, Divine Life is freely bestowed upon and within the hearts, souls, minds, and bodies, too, of all loving, believing and repentant persons who approach Him. He is our God, the Source of all Virtues; and He is one with the Father Who sustains us in existence and with the Holy Spirit Who guides and consoles us. Through our union with Christ, therefore, we share in the life of the Holy Trinity.

- What a pity it is, that so many Catholics don't experience the joy which comes from a grateful realisation that the Holy Sacrifice is offered amidst countless adoring Angels, as Saints and Holy Souls look on in awe and joy; and the outlookers include Christ's Holy Mother, in Heaven, who hopes to be able to greet one day the precious spiritual 'children' whom she now helps by her prayers.

- Who would stay away, if he or she really understood the marvel of the Mass, or recognised the danger of turning one's back on this work of Redemption?

A necessary warning.

- Isn't this the strangest sort of 'secret' - something known but not fully broadcast or realised - that the Act which takes place on our altars is the saving Act to which we can cling in order to be drawn with Christ towards everlasting joy? Shouldn't we broadcast a warning that if we selfishly ignore that Act and ignore the Saviour Whose self-offering for sin it is, we walk away - of our own free will - from penitence, grace and hope, and take the road which can lead nowhere except towards darkness and damnation?

- Anyone who labels this a stern doctrine should realise that it comes from Christ Who is the kindest, gentlest and most loving Friend anyone could have; yet He, being Truth, is of course the most truthful; and nothing He has ever said or that we have ever heard from the Church on which we should rely, or from the Holy Scriptures, or from things written by scholars and Saints, can lead us to think that we can be careless about the danger of leaving Christ: careless about sin. We must never be anything less than perfectly grateful that He holds out to sinful people like ourselves the real hope of living with Him, after our death, in the everlasting bliss of Heaven.

- Faith is essential for an appreciation of the Holy Sacrifice of the Mass. Who except Christ's true believers value the Act and the Person on the altars in our churches and Cathedrals? Yet in every age Christ's sacrifice has been witnessed by a mixed crowd: some people believing, some scoffing, others puzzled or bored or ignorant or impatient. How many of those who listened to Christ in His Earthly life-time or watched Him suffer on the Cross knew that they were present to a life, an Action, a Person and a Sacrifice on which their everlasting joy would depend? Many of them probably saw only a tiresome preacher who was taking foolish risks, and suffered a 'useless' death. What bearing could such a person have on their lives?

- The profound truth which many of us have been privileged to see and to believe is that wherever the Holy Sacrifice of the Mass is offered, souls are saved from danger and are drawn towards Heaven. We need to ask if we and our friends and family are usually moving towards Christ or away from Him.

- It's important that we encourage one another to obey Christ's Commandments and never to shrug aside His wishes. We mustn't judge one another, however, but be compassionate with one another; and meanwhile, we can be sure that Christ can see into every heart. He knows and understands everything, including the reasons why some people accept His gift of faith and ask Him to increase it, whereas other people refuse it. Perhaps we ourselves, with our failings, have helped to make the Church or the Christian Faith seem unattractive; but let's hope that no-one who possesses an ounce of faith or a scrap of interest in the subject will ever become gripped more by his own ambitions than by the hope of eternal joy.

c)   HOW TO BEHAVE IN GOD'S PRESENCE.

A reverent, holy People?

When we're thinking about the salvation which is held out to us through Christ, it's sensible to consider not just the supreme importance of the Mass, but also the manner in which the Holy Sacrifice is offered in our churches.

It's very important that we offer a warm welcome to our brothers and sisters in Christ. It's important that the readings from the Holy Scriptures can be plainly heard. The Word of God in Holy Scripture has been the Church's offering to the faithful for many centuries; and it's the Holy Spirit Who has shaped our liturgy in the living and Sacred Tradition of the Church and Who opens the hearts of listeners. It's very important that both children and adults have been instructed in the meaning of the Mass: that we are taught that the very Word of God Who enlightens our minds in Holy Scripture is made Really Present at the Consecration; and that, of course, is why we should try to make a good preparation.

How many of Christ's People prepare for Mass and Holy Communion by a sincere confession, in the sacrament of Reconciliation? How many of us unfailingly approach Christ with due reverence, and with a determination to give Him first place in our lives, since His life was offered, freely, for each one of us? How many of us always keep the fast, wear suitable clothing in church, respect and help the priests from whom we receive the Lord's Body, and offer sincere prayers for the whole Church: especially for the Holy Father and for all the Bishops who guide us in the Faith?

As must surely be plain by now, the liturgy of the Church is so holy that we should try to walk and move and speak in church in a fitting manner. It's important that we know how to behave in God's presence: with courteous bows and graceful genuflections. Such things as these are practised avidly by people who hear that they've been invited to meet 'Royalty' but are rather neglected by those who, probably through ignorance, enter a church as if entering a dance-hall or a lounge. Meanwhile, we can all aim to be more and more reverent towards God - and charitable and kind towards our brothers and sisters.

A prayerful intention.

What 'counts' above all, as we participate in the Mass, is our union with Christ. It's a praiseworthy thing merely to be present there in obedience to God's wish as expressed through His Church; yet it's much more praiseworthy and beneficial to be of one heart and mind with Christ during His offering. It's supremely important that we unite ourselves, by a sincere and prayerful intention, with Our Lord Jesus Christ: with Him Whose Act of Sacrifice - offered there before us - wins salvation for us who put our trust in Him and repent of our sins. As we unite ourselves with Christ and with His total offering we are one with Him before the Father; and *"the lives of the faithful"* - which are our hearts, our lives, our sufferings and our hopes, with our work and our praises and all of the good things we do, and offer to God - *"acquire a new value"* (CCC:1368).

If eyes could see this.

Faith is so important, for our prayers and devotions, as well as love, that perhaps I can 'illustrate' that faith, in a few sentences, in a further attempt to share some good news about the Mass: about the wonder of the Celebration.

Whoever believes that the Mass is something merely-human will never grasp the wonder and majesty of it. It's not something tedious and repetitive as a theatre-performance can become merely repetitive, or as a gathering with friends can become tedious if we become impatient with human imperfections and with other sources of irritation. No matter how great the imperfections of those who celebrate each Mass, it is, in itself, something holy and beautiful, awesome and effective: all because it is God's work. Since Christ our God is Present during the Mass in an extraordinary way, we who believe that He is Present know that we're immensely privileged to be able to take part; and I'm certain that whoever is willing to believe that the Mass is God's work and worship, and is willing to pray every word of the Mass with sincerity and love, and is willing to feed on Christ, and to serve Christ in everyday life, will grow in faith, and will come to see the truth of the word-picture which now follows.

If people were shown, for an instant - whilst still on Earth - the holiness of the church which has been consecrated and made ready for the Offering of the Holy Sacrifice, and if they could see the dazzling glory and astounding purity of the Holy Saviour Who stands before them after the Consecration, and if they could see the thousands of Saints on high who are waiting with bated breath for Christ to offer His Sacrifice to the Father, and if they could see the Holy Angels poised - in their thousands - to bow down low before the Precious Blood of Christ upon the altar, and if they had any inkling of the torment which Christ endured for each one of us, to save us from estrangement from God our Father - from damnation - and if they had any idea of the never-ending bliss of the Divine Love into which Christ is drawing all who cling to Him and who unite themselves to His Offering of praise, thanks, reparation and trust, and if they could see the Holy and Immaculate Virgin - in Heaven now - who is thrilled by the devotion of all who love her Divine Son, and if they really believed in the Life and the Power of the Most Holy Spirit, Who is at work at the Consecration just as powerfully as He was at work in Our Lady's Immaculate Conception and the Incarnation of Christ within her womb, they would cry out loud: "I'm not worthy to stand in your presence, Lord".

So great would be their longing to be involved in such marvels, in such wonderful and loving Heavenly Company, and with such extraordinary benefits to be gained from sincere participation, and such peace and joy to be accepted from their kind and tender

Saviour in Holy Communion, that they would be willing to fast, pray, wash, confess their sins, do penance gladly and even walk many miles (were they able) in order to attend such an event in such a holy place; and - given the opportunity - they would count themselves privileged to be able to attend not only regularly, but daily, if possible, and even more than once daily.

It's the Will of God that we live 'by faith' whilst on this Earth, as the Church teaches us; but since so many people declare themselves to be unwilling to live by faith and are unwilling to pray or do penance, many have no clear idea of the meaning of the great Event in which they reluctantly participate, Sunday by Sunday. Yet all that I've written above is true; and if this little effort makes anyone take even a scrap more interest in the Holy Sacrifice of the Mass, which is offered at altars all over our country (in this very week, on this very day: and you could go, and listen and pray) I shall thank God once again, for having given me faith, and for having given me the opportunity to share it.

Sinners or Saints?

Perhaps some of you are still wondering why regular Mass attendance is required of us by Christ if we're baptised, and make reasonable efforts to lead good lives. Some of you might say: "Need I humble myself, before God, if I belong to Him as His child: if I'm really adopted, as you say, through Christ? Can't I just rejoice in my new way of life, being kind to everyone, relaxing in God's care, and praying by His sanctuary whenever I feel like doing so, carefree and unafraid?"

What a wonderful picture is painted in these phrases - of an innocent state in which we see purity and confidence combined, with hope reigning supreme in someone who can turn to God in real trust and unselfconscious joy; yet how many people have attained this state? Who amongst us can gaze into the eyes of Our Lord, all our sins not just forgiven but forgotten, and all hint of rebellion or disobedience stilled and utterly forsworn, forever? Only the true saints amongst us, surely: those who are known to God alone and who are 'ripe' for Heaven.

The rest of us, meanwhile, ought to kneel at Mass weekly, as the Church requests, if not daily ... to pray with the sort of hearts which please God most: with contrite hearts, as we yearn to be worthy of Heaven. We believe ourselves privileged, meanwhile, to be allowed to enter God's holy places on Earth, which are places 'set apart' for what is accurately called 'Divine' worship.

All who love God and who love and understand the Mass to some degree know that whenever the Mass is celebrated, worship is offered by God to God, in God. It is offered by Christ to the Father, by the power of the Holy Spirit; and this astonishing worship takes place in our midst because of Christ's great love for us: love most lavishly demonstrated when He sacrificed His life on the Cross because of our sins; and He has left us a living memorial of that love. He allows His unique Sacrifice of love to be offered by our priest at the altar.

What a marvel it is, that Christ Himself - 'whole and entire' - is Really Present before us. How astonishing it is that He allows Himself to be given to each one of us when we receive Him as our spiritual food, and when we rest in the wonderful company of this most intimate and loving friend, in Holy Communion.

May each one of us be propelled into daily life transparent with Christ's love and kindness. May we live for God, and never sin against Him. May we love our neighbour, forgiving as readily as God forgives us. May we 'pray without ceasing'. May we be strong in faith, whether we live in turmoil or calm. May we be grateful for all good things. May the Holy Spirit help us to persevere to the end, leading us, through Christ, to the Father. May we join Christ our Lord, and His beloved Mother, with all the Holy Angels and Saints, in the eternal praise of God's Glory.

THE MASS

QUOTATIONS FROM THE CATECHISM

THE MASS
QUOTATIONS FROM THE CATECHISM

The Catechism of the Catholic Church is so large, and yet so admirable a resource for us all, that it seems wise to list a few brief quotations, under three main headings, to confirm our doctrine and to encourage further exploration.

a)   OUR SALVATION HISTORY.

Loss and Gain.

What is the Church's teaching about human nature, about sin, and about the death and Resurrection of Jesus?

		CCC
1	We are *"created in God's image and called to know and love him."*	31
2	Our first parents' *"disobedient choice"* had *"tragic consequences."*	391 + 399
3	They lost *"the grace of original holiness"*	399
4	*"Sin came into the world ... so death spread to all men."*	402
5	After the fall, God buoyed up mankind *"by promising redemption."*	55

CCC

6 *"In order to gather together scattered humanity God calls Abraham."* 59

7 *"God would gather all his children into the unity of the Church."* 60

8 *"God formed Israel as his people ... and, through Moses, gave them the Law."* 62

9 *"Through the prophets, God forms his people ... in the expectation of a new and everlasting Covenant intended for all, to be written on their hearts."* 64

10 *"By his Revelation, 'the invisible God ... addresses men ... to invite and receive them into his own company'."* 142

11 *"By faith, man completely submits his intellect and his will to God."* 143

12 *"Faith is ... a personal adherence of man to God ... a free assent to the whole truth that God has revealed."* 150

The incarnate Son of God.

13 *"For a Christian, believing in God cannot be separated from believing in the One sent ... Jesus Christ ... himself God, the Word made flesh."* 151

14 *"Jesus is conceived by the Holy Spirit in the Virgin Mary's womb because he is the New Adam ... 'from Heaven' ... the head of redeemed humanity."* 504

15 *" 'Christ died for our sins'."* 619

CCC

16 *"Jesus atoned for our faults and made satisfaction for our sins to the Father."* 615

17 *"By his loving obedience to the Father, 'unto death, even death on a Cross' (Phil 2:8) Jesus fulfils the atoning mission (cf.Is53:10) of the suffering Servant."* 623

18 *"Christ's Resurrection is ... a transcendent intervention of God himself in creation and history."* 648

19 *" 'as Christ was raised from the dead by the glory of the Father we too might walk in newness of life'."* 654

20 *"this new life is above all justification that reinstates us in God's grace."* 654

21 *"Jesus Christ, having entered the sanctuary of Heaven"* (at His ascension) *"intercedes constantly for us as the mediator who assures us of the permanent outpouring of the Holy Spirit"* 667

---

b) THE SACRAMENT OF OUR SALVATION

An important question.

Christ died nearly 2000 years ago for our sins. How can we 'touch' that event and express our faith in it, as individuals?

CCC

22 *"The Eucharist [is] the sacrament of our Salvation accomplished by Christ on the Cross."* 1359

23	*"The Eucharist is the memorial of Christ's Passover, the making present and the sacramental offering of his unique sacrifice, in the Liturgy"*, which is the public work of the Church which is His Body.	1362
24	*"The memorial"* - the anamnesis - *"is ... the proclamation of the mighty works wrought by God for men. In a liturgical celebration ... they become in a certain way present and real."*	1363
25	*" 'As often as the sacrifice of the Cross ... is celebrated on the altar, the work of our redemption is carried out'."*	1364
26	The Mass is Calvary's sacrifice now: as the Church says: *"a visible sacrifice."*	1366
27	The Mass *"re-presents (makes present) the sacrifice of the cross"* and *"is its memorial"* and *" applies its fruits."*	1366
28	Our priest *"possesses the authority to act in the power and place of the person of Christ Himself."* So the priest, in the person of Christ, uses the power Christ gave, and does what Christ did at the Last Supper.	1548
29	So that Salvation can be brought to us who participate, the priest says: *"This is my body which is given for you,"* and also: *"This cup which is poured out for you is the New Covenant in my blood."*	1365
30	We believe that *"Christ's sacrifice present on the altar makes it possible for all generations to be united with his offering."*	1368

31 *"In the Eucharist Christ gave us the very body which he gave up for us on the Cross, the very blood which he 'poured out for many for the forgiveness of sins'."* 1365

32 *"The Sacrifice of Christ"* on Calvary *"and the sacrifice of the Eucharist are one single sacrifice: 'The Victim is one and the same: the same now offers through the ministry of priests, who then offered himself on the Cross; only the manner of offering is different.' 'In this divine sacrifice which is celebrated in the Mass, the same Christ who offered himself once in a bloody manner on the altar of the Cross is contained and is offered in an unbloody manner'."* 1367

33 *"In the Eucharist the Church is as it were at the foot of the cross with Mary, united with the offering and intercession of Christ;"* and the Church prays to the Father: 'We offer you in thanksgiving this holy and living sacrifice." (Eucharistic Prayer III.) 1370

---

c) THE LIVING BREAD FROM HEAVEN.

Christ Present 'whole and entire'.

What is the Church's sure teaching about the Holy Eucharist, which is both a sacrifice and a sacrament?

CCC

34 *"Jesus said: 'I am the living bread that came down from heaven ... he who eats my flesh and drinks my blood has eternal life and ... abides in me, and I in him'" (Jn 6:51-56)* 1406

35 *"Christ is ... really and mysteriously made present."* 1357

36 *"In the most blessed sacrament of the Eucharist 'the body and blood, together with the soul and divinity of our Lord Jesus Christ and, therefore, the whole Christ, is truly, really and substantially contained.'"* 1374

37 *"By the Consecration of the bread and wine there takes place a change of the whole substance of the bread into the substance of the body of Christ our Lord and of the whole substance of the wine into the substance of his blood. [This change is called] transubstantiation."* 1376

38 *"It is a substantial presence by which Christ, God and man, makes himself wholly and entirely present"* under the continuing appearance of bread and wine 1374

39 *"The Eucharist is also the sacrifice of the Church"* ... which we call *"the Body of Christ ... With him, she herself is offered whole and entire."* 1368

40 *"The lives of the faithful, their praise, sufferings, prayer and work, are united with those of Christ ... and so acquire a new value."* 1368

41 We pray for the Pope, for our Bishop, and for all priests, deacons and faithful, united with *"those already in the glory of Heaven."* 1370

CCC

42 *"The Eucharistic sacrifice is also offered for the faithful departed who ... 'are not yet wholly purified'."*... 1371

Worship of the Eucharist.

43 *"In the liturgy of the Mass we express our faith in the real presence of Christ under the species of bread and wine by ... genuflecting or bowing deeply as a sign of adoration of the Lord. 'The Catholic Church ... still offers to the sacrament of the Eucharist the cult of adoration not only during the Mass, but also outside of it, reserving the consecrated hosts with the utmost care, exposing them to the solemn veneration of the faithful, and carrying them in procession'."* 1378

44 *"The tabernacle should be located in an especially worthy place in church, and should be constructed in such a way that it emphasises and manifests the truth of the real presence of Christ in the Blessed Sacrament."* 1379

45 *"Anyone conscious of a grave sin must receive the sacrament of Reconciliation before coming to communion."* 1385

46 About Holy Communion: *"To respond to this invitation we must prepare ourselves for so great a grace and so holy a moment"* so that we are not *"'guilty of profaning the body and blood of the Lord'."* 1385

47 *"Bodily demeanour (gestures, clothing) ought to convey the respect, solemnity and joy of this moment when Christ becomes our guest."* 1387

The Eucharist: the sacrifice of the Church.

CCC

48 *"The Eucharist ... re-presents (makes present) the sacrifice of the Cross."* 1366

49 *"The sacrifice Christ offered once for all on the Cross remains ever present."* 1364

50 *"The Eucharist is a sacrifice of thanksgiving to the Father ... by which the Church expresses her gratitude to God for all his benefits."* 1360

51 *"The Eucharist is also a sacrifice of praise by which the Church sings the glory of God in the name of all creation."* 1361

52 *"This sacrifice of praise is possible only through Christ: he unites the faithful to his person, to his praise, and to his intercession, so that the sacrifice of praise to the Father is offered through Christ and with him, to be accepted in him,"* because of His merits and His headship of the Church and of mankind 1361

The Eucharist and the unity of Christians.

CCC

53 *"The Eastern Churches that are not in full communion with the Catholic Church celebrate the Eucharist with great love. 'These Churches, although separated from us, yet possess true sacraments, above all - by apostolic succession - the priesthood and the Eucharist, whereby they are still joined to us in closest intimacy.' A certain communion in sacris, and so in the Eucharist, 'given suitable circumstances and the approval of Church authority, is not merely possible but is encouraged.' "* 1399

54 *Ecclesial communities derived from the Reformation and separated from the Catholic Church 'have not preserved the proper reality of the Eucharistic mystery in its fullness, especially because of the absence of the sacrament of Holy Orders.' It is for this reason that Eucharistic intercommunion with these communities is not possible for the Catholic Church. However these ecclesial communities, 'when they commemorate the Lord's death and resurrection in the Holy Supper ... profess that it signifies life in communion with Christ and await his coming in glory.' "* 1400

55 *When, in the Ordinary's judgement, a grave necessity arises, Catholic ministers may give the sacraments of Eucharist, Penance, and Anointing of the Sick to other Christians not in full communion with the Catholic Church, who ask for them of their own will, provided they give evidence of holding the Catholic faith regarding these sacraments, and possess the required dispositions."* 1401

THE MASS

USEFUL SCRIPTURE REFERENCES

THE MASS

USEFUL SCRIPTURE REFERENCES

a) THE OLD TESTAMENT.

Our First Parents' rebellion	Gn 3:6-10
God's covenant with Noah	Gn 9:1-13
God's promise to Abram	Gn 15:1-6
God's Covenant with Abram	Gn 17:1-22
The Passover celebration	Ex 12
God's Covenant with Moses and the people	Ex 19:3-8
The Commandments	Ex 20:1-21
The tablets of the Law	Ex 34:1-35
Moses' words about keeping God's "LAWS AND CUSTOMS"	Dt 4:4-10
Moses' words about teaching the children	Dt 6:1-13
God's glory fills the Temple	2 Ch 7:1-22
About God's judgement: how "GOD WEIGHS THE HEART"	Pr 21:2-3
Isaiah's words about "A MAN OF SORROWS ... CRUSHED FOR OUR SINS"	Is 52:13 -53:12
God's words about a new Covenant, by which: "DEEP WITHIN THEM I WILL PLANT MY LAW, WRITING IT ON THEIR HEARTS."	Jr 31:31-34
Ezekiel's words about God as Shepherd	Ezk 34:1-10
A prophesy about how dry bones shall live	Ezk 37:1-14
Words about living water from the Temple which would later flow from Christ's side on the Cross	Ezk 47:1-12
Daniel's vision of the Ancient of Days and of "ONE LIKE A SON OF MAN"	Dn 7:9-14
Zechariah's prophesy about "YOUR KING [COMING] TO YOU ... ON A DONKEY" - about Christ's humility	Zc 9:9-10

USEFUL SCRIPTURE REFERENCES (Continued)

b) THE NEW TESTAMENT.

The Beatitudes: a picture of holiness	Mt 5:3-11
Christ's advice about reconciliation with our neighbour "LEAVE YOUR GIFT AT THE ALTAR"	Mt 5:23-24
A warning about: "BE CAREFUL NOT TO PARADE YOUR GOOD DEEDS BEFORE MEN."	Mt 6:1-4
Christ's words about how "IT IS NOT THOSE WHO SAY TO ME, 'LORD, LORD,' WHO WILL ENTER THE KINGDOM OF HEAVEN, BUT THE PERSON WHO DOES THE WILL OF MY FATHER IN HEAVEN"	Mt 7:21-23
Christ's words about being "WORTHY OF ME", and about how each of us must "TAKE UP HIS CROSS"	Mt 10:37-39
The miracle of the loaves (about a year before the Last Supper)	Mt 14:15-21
Christ's encouraging words about a "MUSTARD SEED" of faith	Mt 17:20
St. Matthew's account of the New Covenant meal	Mt 26:26-29
The risen Christ: living Lord, worshipped	Mt 28:17
Christ's command about teaching His commands to all	Mt 28:19-20
Christ's promise: "I AM WITH YOU ALWAYS ..."	Mt 28:20
Christ's words about eating His flesh: in order to have life	Jn 6:52-58
Christ's declaration about "WHEN I AM LIFTED UP FROM THE EARTH, I SHALL DRAW ALL MEN TO MYSELF"	Jn 12:32
Christ's Last Discourse	Jn Chs 13-1
Christ's declaration that "CUT OFF FROM ME YOU CAN DO NOTHING"	Jn 15:5
An enquiry to Peter, in the early Church: "WHAT MUST WE DO" (to be saved)	Ac 2:37
A description of how the early Christians "REMAINED FAITHFUL TO THE TEACHING OF THE APOSTLES, TO THE BROTHERHOOD, TO THE BREAKING OF BREAD, AND TO THE PRAYERS."	Ac 2:42

USEFUL SCRIPTURE REFERENCES (Continued)

St. Paul's declaration that "WE WERE RECONCILED TO GOD BY THE DEATH OF HIS SON"	Ro 5:10
Reassurance that: "YOU, GOD HAS MADE MEMBERS OF CHRIST JESUS AND ... HE HAS BECOME OUR WISDOM, AND OUR VIRTUE, AND OUR HOLINESS, AND OUR FREEDOM."	1 Co 1:30
St. Paul's account of the 'SINGLE BODY' we become, as we receive the body of Christ	1 Co 10:16-17
St. Paul's declaration that in the Eucharist "YOU ARE PROCLAIMING HIS DEATH."	1 Co 11:26-27
St. Paul's words about unworthy Communions	1 Co 11:27
Love, according to St. Paul	1 Co 13:4-7
About not "WATERING DOWN THE WORD OF GOD," but rather, of learning to "RADIATE THE LIGHT OF THE KNOWLEDGE OF GOD'S GLORY"	2 Co 4:1-6
About how we can "PROVE WE ARE SERVANTS OF GOD"	2 Co 6:4-10
About how "GOD LOVES A CHEERFUL GIVER" who has sympathy and generosity	2 Co 9:6-15
We are chosen by God "TO BE HOLY AND SPOTLESS"	Ep 1:4-7
St. Paul's fervent yearnings, as "THIS, THEN, IS WHAT I PRAY, KNEELING BEFORE THE FATHER"	Ep 3:14
How we should "PRAY ALL THE TIME, ASKING FOR WHAT YOU NEED"	Ep 6:18
About there being "NO NEED TO WORRY"	Ph 4:6-7
A description of Christ as "THE IMAGE OF THE UNSEEN GOD"	Col 1:15-20
A reminder that "YOU ARE GOD'S CHOSEN RACE, HIS SAINTS; HE LOVES YOU"	Col 3:12-17
St. Paul's reminder that "WHAT GOD WANTS IS FOR YOU ALL TO BE HOLY"	1 Th 4:3
St Paul's urgent plea that Christ's friends "STAND FIRM THEN, BROTHERS, AND KEEP THE TRADITIONS THAT WE TAUGHT YOU WHETHER BY WORD OR MOUTH OF BY LETTER"	2 Th 2:15

USEFUL SCRIPTURE REFERENCES (Continued)

St. Paul's further advice about the liturgy, with its "PRAYERS OFFERED FOR EVERYONE" ……………..	1 Tm 2:1
A warning against "POINTLESS PHILOSOPHICAL DISCUSSIONS," and about holding to sound doctrine …...	1 Tm 6:3-6, 20-21
Encouragement that we "KEEP AS YOUR PATTERN THE SOUND TEACHING YOU HAVE HEARD FROM ME" .	2 Tm 1:13-14
A warning, of Christ, that "IF WE DISOWN HIM, THEN HE WILL DISOWN US" ……………………………………..	2 Tm 2:8-13
A description of Christ as "THE RADIANT LIGHT OF GOD'S GLORY" who is now "IN HEAVEN" …………..	Hb 1:3-4
A new Covenant …………………………………………	Heb 8:6-13
About perseverance in the Faith, throughout all sufferings …..	Hb 10:32-3
About how "IF ANYONE OF YOU IS IN TROUBLE, HE SHOULD PRAY" …………………………………….	Jm 5:13-18
An incentive to stop behaving indecently: a consideration of "WHAT CHRIST SUFFERED IN THIS LIFE" …………..	1 P 4:1-4
"GOD IS LOVE" …………………………………………..	1 Jn 4:16

****

"I tell you most solemnly,
if you do not eat the flesh of the Son of Man
and drink his blood,
you will not have life in you.
Anyone who does eat my flesh and drink my blood
has eternal life,
and I shall raise him up on the last day.
For my flesh is real food
and my blood is real drink.
He who eats my flesh and drinks my blood
lives in me
and I live in him.
As I, who am sent by the living Father,
myself draw life from the Father,
so whoever eats me will draw life from me.
This is the bread come down from heaven;
not like the bread our ancestors ate:
they are dead,
but anyone who eats this bread will live for ever."

(Jn 6:53-58)

DETAILS ABOUT THE COMPANY "RADIANT LIGHT".

The writings and paintings of Elizabeth Wang are published by **Radiant Light**

Radiant Light is a non-profit making company. It has wide trading objects, together with two specific aims which are:

> *'For the glory of God the Most Holy Trinity, for the honour of the Blessed Virgin Mary, and out of love for the Catholic Church and loyalty to the Pope:*

(1) to advance the Roman Catholic religion
(2) to promote the works of Elizabeth Wang

Please write to the Harpenden address below if you would like to be put on the mailing list.

If you would like to help support the work of Radiant Light, please send a UK cheque to **Radiant Light, 25 Rothamsted Avenue, Harpenden, Herts, AL5 2DN., U.K.**

Cheques must be made payable to 'Radiant Light'. Thank you.

Company No. 3701357 (Company limited to guarantee and not having a share capital).

Visit the Radiant Light web-site at:
www.radiantlight.org.uk

Book Orders and Distribution.

Radiant Light books, photographs and posters are available from St. Pauls book shop next to Westminster Cathedral, London:

St. Pauls
(By Westminster Cathedral)
Morpeth Terrace
Victoria
London SW1P 1EP
United Kingdom.

Tel: 020 7828 5582
Fax: 020 7828 3329

email: bookshop@stpauls.org.uk

Mail-Order: If you would like to order Radiant Light works through the post, St Pauls has a very efficient *mail-order service,* which will send your order throughout the UK and anywhere in the world. Please telephone St Pauls and ask them how you may order Radiant Light books. *But please do not send money or orders until you have been in touch with them.*